MW00948563

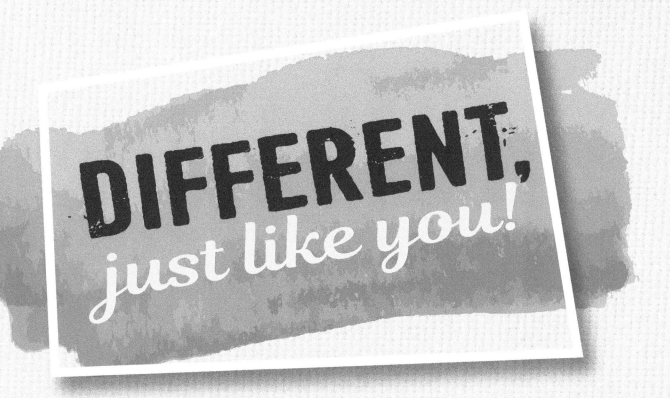

DIFFERENT,
just like you!

By **Teska T. Frisby**
Proud daughter of Ruth DeCosta and Charles Flowers Sr.

Illustrated By **Kal'El Livingston**

Copyright 2021 by Teska T. Frisby
All rights reserved. This book or part thereof may not be reproduced in
any form without permission in writing from the publisher, Pink Butterfly Press LLC.
www.PinkButterflyPressLLC.com

The copying, scanning, uploading, and/or distribution of this book
via internet, social media, or any other means without written permission
of the publisher is illegal and punishable by law.

Please only purchase authorized electronic editions,
and please do not participate in or encourage electronic piracy.

Hardback ISBN: 978-1-63795-396-9
Paperback ISBN: 979-8-7033-8881-5

Pink Butterfly Press
Publishing for the next generation

Looking at the world through the eyes of someone with special needs will hopefully open our eyes to their world. All of us need someone, **although** some of us rely on others more than most. We don't all love the same way, but we all desire love and to be loved by others.

To my inspiration, Samuel (Desi) T. Frisby Jr., I praise and thank God for giving you to us. You erase the word can't from our dictionary!

To my amazing husband, Samuel T. Frisby Sr., your love helps make mornings a lot brighter! To our son, Theodore Terrence Barak Frisby, **you** are a gift that has no end. Your father and I are grateful that God gave you to us. To our nephew, David Catanch, thank you for motivating me to get this book out of my head and onto paper!

To my incredible village: Momma LaLove (Jeannine F. LaRue) and Miss Kia M. Kelley, thank you for your awesome time, input, and guidance. I love you both to the Moon and back.

Most of all, to our Lord and Savior Jesus Christ, I pray You are pleased with our worship!

When I wake up each morning and open my eyes, WOW, I am so excited to start each day! Mom usually wakes me with a kiss and then says, "Good morning, Samuel. How are you this morning?" Then we make our way to the bathroom, just like you, to get washed up for the day. Mom holds my hand to guide me to the bathroom, and although this may seem different, I still need to get washed. It's different, but I'm just like you!

Back to my room we go to pick out my clothes for the day. Decisions, decisions! Mom goes into my closet and shows me some tops and bottoms. After a few selections, I pick out what I want to wear. Yes, Mom must get my clothes from the closet for me, and that might be different from you getting your clothes out, but I still want to help decide what I want to wear. It is a little different, but I'm just like you!

It is time to put on my clothes. I do this one leg at a time and one arm at a time. Although Mom must help me get my clothes on, I still need to get dressed, which may be different, but I'm just like you!

Off to the kitchen we go for breakfast. Dad comes to help guide me as I walk down the stairs. You see, if I do not have someone to guide me, I might fall. Like you, I need to make my way to the kitchen table, but it may take me a little more time. Different, but I'm just like you!

It is time to eat, YES! Mealtimes are some of my favorite parts of my day! After Dad helps me sit in my seat at the table, we hold hands, and Dad says grace. When prayer is over, Dad leans over to my plate and cuts my food. I sit and eat my food at the table with my family, a little differently, but I still must eat, JUST like you!

When it is time to go to school, Dad gets my coat from the closet and lays it on my bed. I say, "I can do it, I can do it," and Dad lets me put on my jacket by myself. It takes a little more time for me to get my jacket on and then zip it up, but eventually I get it done, a little slower and differently, but I still get it done, just like you do!

When I am in class, I love to learn. Two of my favorite subjects are math and language arts. When my teacher asks a question, I don't shout out the answer. I raise my hand and wait until I'm called on. Not at all different. I'm just like you!

Sometimes, my family goes to the mall. My dad usually pushes me in my special stroller. My stroller helps me get from place to place more comfortably. We might go into a restaurant while at the mall. Sometimes, people stop and stare at me. I'm never sure why they are staring. I am spending quality time with my family. That's not so different, it's just like them!

On Sunday afternoons, we usually go to my Mimi's
(my grandmother's) house. Mimi makes some of the best
shrimp, baked chicken, and asparagus. Yum, yum!
(She also gives some of the best hugs in the world!)
It's no different from your grandma or grandpa.
I love my grandparents too, just like you do!

If I get a cold or get sick, it's off to the doctor's office I go. My doctor examines me and checks my temperature. Sometimes, I must take medicine to help me get better (yuck), just like you do!

There are times when I get sad. If someone yells or is mean, it hurts my feelings. Sometimes, I cry in silence, and sometimes, I cry out loud. I have feelings and need to express them. I'm just like you!

If I fall, I must call out for help.
When my mom or dad comes to help me get up,
they hug me and ask me if I am okay. I am thankful for
my parents' love. JUST like YOU!

When we are in the van together, my family tells jokes sometimes. We can get silly, and I join in. When I speak, they must listen more closely, but I have something to say. My humor might be a little different, but I like to laugh, just like you!

When it is time to go home, my brother, Theo, helps me get inside the van. He usually helps me walk to the stairs once we get to our house. Theo or my cousin, David, usually unlocks the door, and then one of them will guide me into the house by holding my hand. We always make it back safely. A little different, but I'm just like you!

In the evening, it's quiet time. My brother or my cousin comes into my room and reads with me, and sometimes they might even read to me. I love it when they come in and spend time with me. It shows me that they care. I like reading books and spending time with family, just like you do!

On my sixteenth birthday, I finally got to do what my great-uncle Thomas DeCosta and my great-grandma Susie Frisby did, preach! My grandpa and grandma Hinmon let me preach in their pulpit. I was so excited to have one of my dreams come true, like you would be excited to have one of your dreams come true. That may be different, but I'm just like you!

Do you have big dreams? Ever since I was four years old, I wanted to be an ordained preacher. Well, guess what? On November 3, 2019, Bishop Earl E. Jenkins ordained me as a licensed preacher! I had waited all my life for that day, and it happened! My ministry may be different from others, but God can, and does use me. JUST LIKE HE CAN USE YOU!

Just before I go to sleep, I say a prayer to thank God for my day. I thank Him for my parents, my family, and my friends. I especially thank Him for giving me life, and I ask Him to keep us all safe. I know God hears me because even though I am different, He loves me, just like He loves you!

So, if you see me out and about, do not stare, or point, or even whisper and think that I don't care. I am human, and I am enjoying my life. God put me here with a purpose to fulfill, and just as it says in Philippians 4:13, I can do all things through Christ which strengthens me! God made me and He made you too, just as we are. That makes us perfect, and I believe this is true!

THE MORAL OF THIS STORY IS:

It does not matter how tall or how short you are. It does not matter if you are heavy or thin. It does not matter what your ethnicity is or even your religion! We all want love. And we all desire to give love. We all bleed the same red blood.
We all have family and friends to whom we show our emotions. We all do the same things, sometimes in a different language or a different manner, but the sentiment is the same.
We all want our families to be safe, prosperous, and to feel loved and secure.

So, the next time you see someone who does not look like those in your home, do not treat them with disdain or disrespect. Although they might look, sound, and play differently, they are human beings, JUST like YOU!

REFLECTIONS:

While navigating this life, I have noticed that we all are making an impression on everyone we encounter. Even when we are not trying to, or paying attention to our surroundings, we are still influencing those in our midst.

The world would be a little better, a little kinder, and a little lighter if we made a conscious decision to care about those who are a little different. They do not want to be seen any differently than anyone else. They might be different, but they are just like you.

BE BLESSED, HEALTHY, AND EXCITED!

THE END.

CPSIA information can be obtained
at www.ICGtesting.com
Printed in the USA
BVHW021230270221
601299BV00013B/89